COSMOPOLITAN COMPUTERS FOR BASIC SCHOOLS
@ Olushola Samuel Adedokun 2022

Cosmopolitan Computer Books Series (Book 2)
Divine Connection Publishers,
Challenge, Off Ring Road, Ibadan, Oyo State, Nigeria.
via Amazon Kindle Direct Publishing

Tel Nos: +234 8034650934, 08084507132; 08166705190

ISBN:

Printed & Published by:
AMAZON KINDLE DIRECT PUBLISHING

Contents

Preface

Cosmopolitan Computer Book is a series of six books written to cover current Universal Basic Education (UBE)/NERDC Curriculum on Computer Education and meant to prepare pupils for the study of computer.

The first series - Books 1, 2 & 3 are meant for the Lower Basic Education, which are full of fascinating pictures with educative interpretation and exercises to prepare pupils for future success.

The second series consisting of Books 4, 5 & 6 are meant for Middle Basic Education. They are clearly illustrated with simple language which is easy to read.

Thus, it is no doubt that these Computer Books will develop pupils and make them cosmopolitan as far as computer education is concerned. It will also be useful for teachers to enhance effective teaching of computer studies in the primary schools.

- ***Author***

CHAPTER ONE

Description of Computer

Computer is an electronic machine

Computer accepts DATA

Computer processes DATA

Computer generates useful INFORMATION.

Computer accepts DATA through INPUT DEVICES

e.g.

Keyboard

  ***Mouse***

 ***Scanner,*** etc

Computer processes DATA through

PROCESSING UNITS e.g.

 ***Central Processing Unit (CPU),***

Computer generates INFORMATION through
OUTPUT DEVICES e.g.

Monitor

Printer

Speaker, etc

<u>**Class Activity**</u>

Answer all the following questions

1. Computer is an __ machine.

     (a) light

     (b) electronic

     (c) spinning

2. Computer makes use of ______ to work.

     (a) candle

     (b) fuel

     (c) electricity

3. Computer processes data through ______ device.

     (a) Input

     (b) Processing

     (c) Output

4. Computer accepts data through ________ device.

     (a) Output

     (b) Input

     (c) processing

5. ______ is an example of Input Device.

     (a) Speaker

(b) Mouse

(c) Monitor

6. ___________ is an example of Output Device.

(a) Monitor

(b) Joystick

(c) Light Pen

Mark (√) the right box YES   NO

7.   is an example of Output Device. YES   NO

8.   is an example of Input Device. YES   NO

9.   is an example of Input Device. YES   NO

10.   is an example of Input Device. YES   NO

<u>*Practical Class 1*</u>

Trace the picture below with Pencil and color it

MONITOR (LCD)

This is a Monitor.

It has a Power B___________

It also has a S___________

I can trace it with my pencil.

I can color it with my crayon.

Marks: ___________

Practical Class 2

Trace the picture below with Pencil and color it

This is a Printer.

It is used to print our D___________

It also has a Paper T___________

I can trace it with my pencil.

I can color it with my crayon.

Marks: ___________

CHAPTER TWO

Computerized Electronic Devices

Computerized electronic devices are devices that make use of electricity. They work faster and easier when they are powered up by electricity.

The following are the examples of Computerized Electronic Devices:

Electronic Calculator

Digital Wristwatch

Washing Machine

Organizer

Liquid Dispenser

Pager

Electric Iron

Fax Machine

Refrigerator

<u>Class Activity</u>

Answer the following questions

1. Computerized Devices make use of __ to function.

   (a) fuel

   (b)   water

   (c)   electricity

2. Computerized Devices work _______.

   (a) slow

   (b) faster

   (c) without human intervention

3. _______ is an example of Computerized Devices.

   (a) Washing Machine

   (b) Blackboard

   (c) Table

4. Liquid Dispenser and Fax Machine are

examples of ___ Devices.

(a) Magnetic

(b) Computerized

(c) Speedy

5. Computerized Devices are used in many

homes. YES or NO

6. _________ is an example of Computerized Devices.

(a) fuel

(b) Petrol

(c) electric iron

7. _______is among the computerized devices.

(a) Refrigerator

(b) Car Battery

(c) Spaghetti

Read the following loudly

8.   What is this?

    It is a Washing Machine

9.   What is this?

    It is a Digital Wrist watch

10.   What is this?

    It is a Pager

11.   What is this?

    It is a Refrigerator

12.   What is this?

    It is an Electric Iron

Now fill in the missing gap

13. 

This is a ____________

    (a)   Washing Machine

    (b)   Digital Wrist watch

    (c)   pager

14. 

This is a _________

    (a)   Digital Wrist watch

    (b)   Washing Machine

    (c)   pager

15. 

This is a _________

    (a)   Pager

    (b)   Washing Machine

    (c)   Digital Wrist watch

<u>***Practical Class 1***</u>

Trace the picture below with Pencil and color it

Washing Machine

This is a ________________

It is a Computerized D__________

It uses E__________

I can trace it with my pencil.

I can color it with my crayon.

Marks: ____________

CHAPTER THREE

Parts of Computer System

The Computer System has many parts. Below are the pictures of the parts of Computer System;

White Monitor (Monochrome)

Colour Monitor (Multichrome)

Compact Disc/ Diskette

Keyboard

Compact Disc ROM

Scanner

Desktop (Mini Tower) CPU

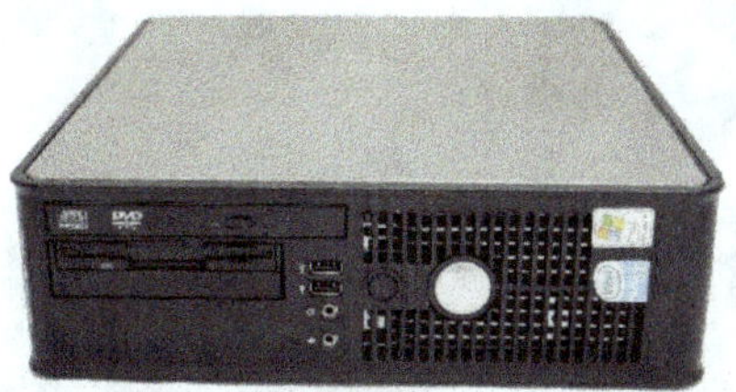

Desktop (Flat Top) CPU

Hard Disk

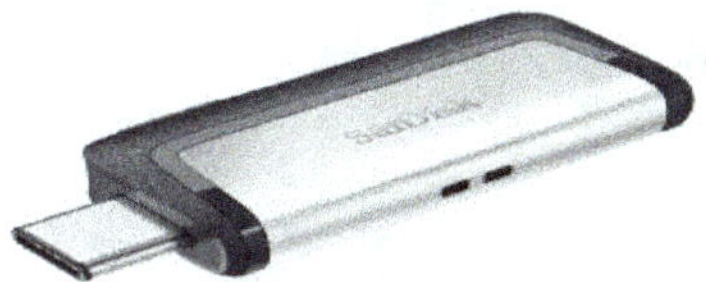

Flash Drive

Memory Cards

HP LaserJet Printer

Mini Computer (Laptop)

Joystick

Uninterrupted Power Supply (UPS)

Class Activity

Complete each of the sentences below

(1)   This is a ________

    (a)   Monitor

    (b)   Scanner

    (c)   Keyboard

(2)   This is a __________

    (a)   Scanner

    (b)   Hard Disk

    (c)   Compact Disc

(3)   This is a ________

    (a)   Printer

    (b)   Compact Disc

    (c)   Cassettee

(4)    This is a _________

    (a)   Memory Card

    (b)   Monitor

    (c)   Sewing Machine

(5)   This is a __________

    (a)   CPU

    (b)   Flash

    (c)   Drive

Class Activity

Join the right picture with the right word

(Use pencil)

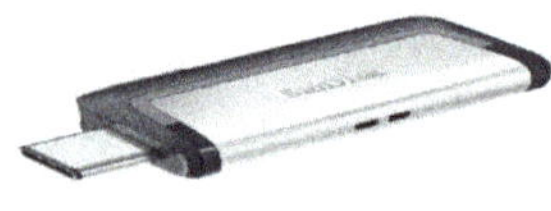

Joystick

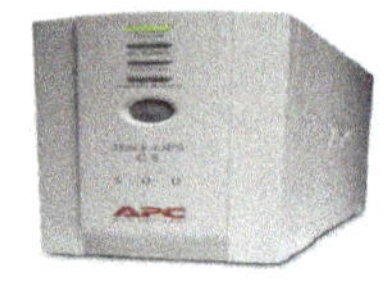

Laptop

Uninterupted Power Supply

Desktop

Memory Card

Printer

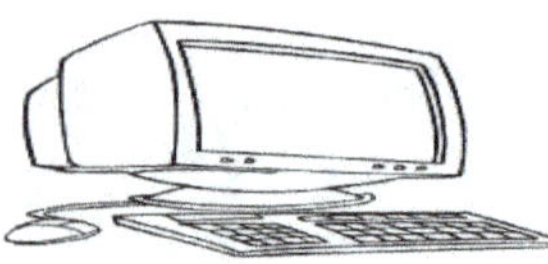

Flash Drive

<u>*Practical Class*</u>

Draw the Computer Monitor below with your Pencil

This is Computer Monitor

It is a Mono___________ Monitor

It can only display One C__________

I can trace it with my pencil.

I can color it with my crayon.

Mark: _______________

<u>*Practical Class*</u>

Draw the Central Processing Unit (CPU) below

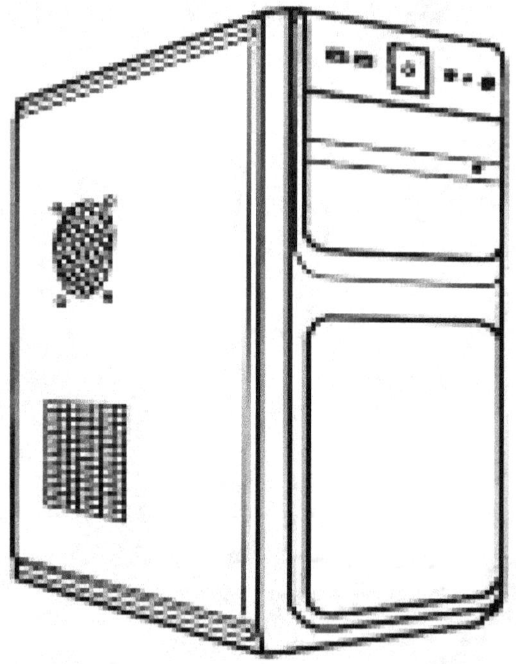

This is Central Processing Unit (CPU)

It has a Disc ____________

It has a power ____________

I can trace it with my pencil.

I can color it with my crayon.

Mark: ____________

CHAPTER FOUR

What Parts of Computer Look Like

Each of the part of computer looks like something.

Let examine what each of these parts of computer

looks like:

Monitor looks like a **Television Set**

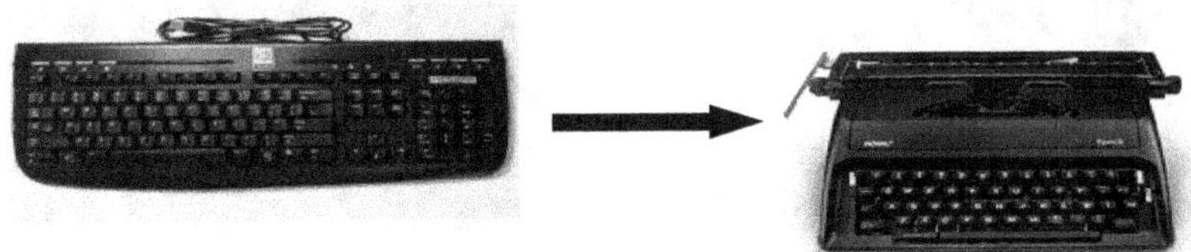

Keyboard looks like **Typewriting Machine or
a calculator**

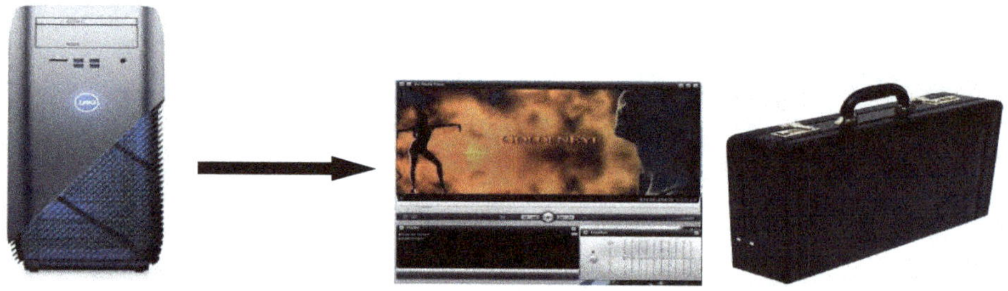

CPU looks like *Video Player* or *Brief Case*

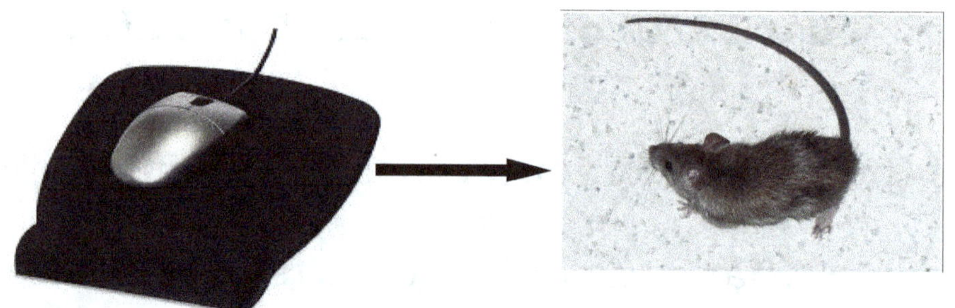

Mouse looks like *a rat moving on a table or Toilet Soap*

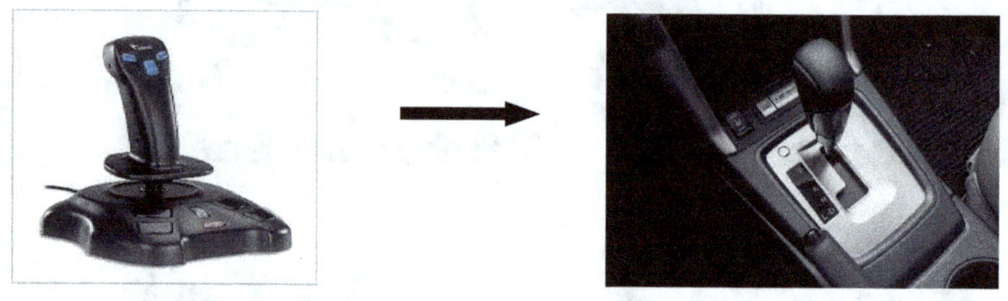

Joystick looks like *a Video Game Pad*

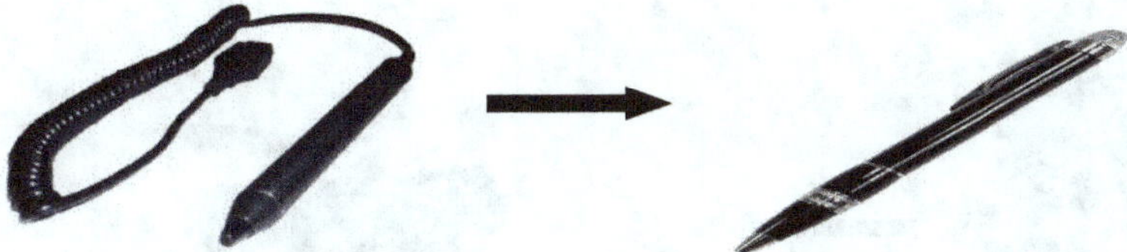

Light Pen looks like **a Pen**

Diskette looks like **a Video or Radio Cassette**

Compact Disc looks like **Stereo Disc**

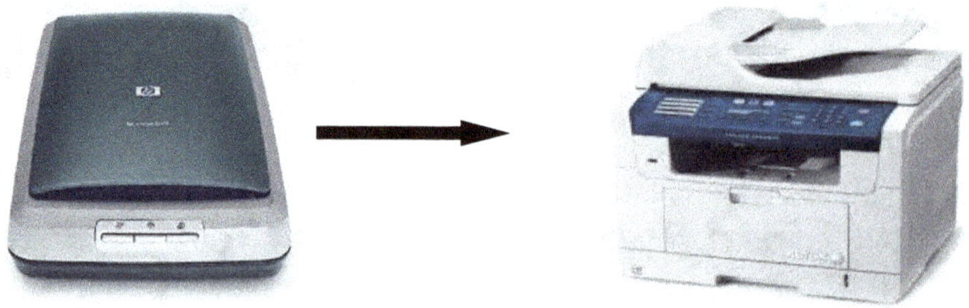

The Scanner looks like **a Photocopy Machine**

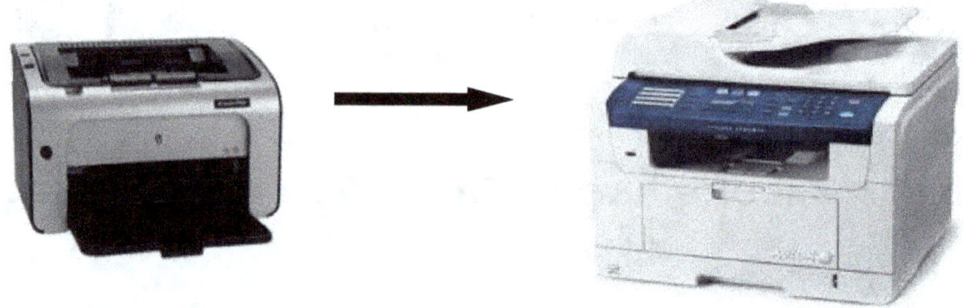

The Printer also looks like a **Photocopy Machine**

<u>**Class Activity**</u>

Underline the right option from the options labeled (a) - (c) below

(1) Monitor look like ____________

    (a) Soap

    (b) Television Set

    (c) Ball

(2) ________ looks like a rat moving on a table

    (a) Keyboard

    (b) Mouse

    (c) Typewriter

(3) CPU looks like ________

    (a) Brief Case

    (b) Photocopy Machine

    (c) Table

(4)   Keyboard looks like __________

(a) hand

(b) Typewriter

(c) Video Player

(5)   Compact Disc look like a __________

(a) Motor

(b) Rat

(c) Stereo Disc

(6)   Joystick looks like a __________

(a) Banana

(b) Car Gear

(c)   Bell

(7)   ______________ looks like a Rat

(a) Keyboard

(b) Monitor

(c) Stereo Disc

(8) ____________ looks Joystick.

    (a) Banana

    (b) Car Gear

    (c) Bell

Answer YES or NO

(9)   looks like a Biro or Pencil.

    (a) Yes

    (b) No

(10)   looks like a Television Set.

    (a) Yes

    (b) No

(11) Keyboard looks like a   .

    (a) Yes

    (b) No

(12)  looks like Gear of a car.

(a) Yes

(b) No

(13) 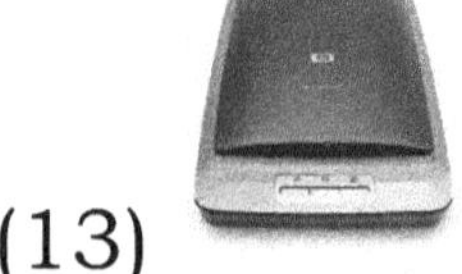 looks like a Brief Case.

(a) Yes

(b) No

(14)  looks like a  .

(a) Yes

(b) No

(15)  looks like a Rat on the table.

(a) Yes

(b) No

<u>Practical Class</u>

Identify the object below

This is Photocopy M________________

It is used to make P __________ of documents

It is like a S__________

I can trace it with my pencil.

I can color it with my crayon.

Mark: ______________

CHAPTER FIVE

Places Where Computer are found

The followings are the places where computer can be found:

Home

School

Church

Hospital

Court

Office

Airport

Banks

Hotel

Art Studio

Mosque

Office

Parliamentary Building

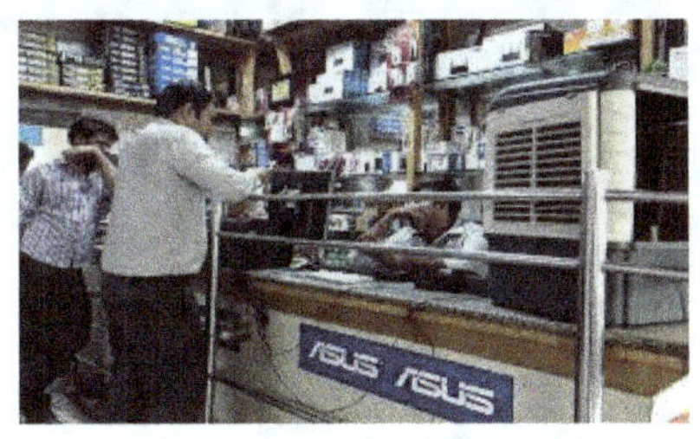

Supermarket

<u>Class Activity</u>

Match each of the pictures below with the right   word

Supermarket

Hospital

Church

School

House

Court

Class Activity

Identify each of the places below:

____

____

____

____

____

<u>**Class Activity**</u>

What do we use computer for in the following places?

1. Computer system is used for ______ in the hospital.

    (a) Killing

    (b) Treatment of patients

    (c) Sweeping floor

2. Computer System is used for the following purposes EXCEPT ______ in the school.
    (a) Treatment of patients
    (b) Keeping of records of students
    (c) Teaching Aid

3. Computer system is used for ______ in the Airport.
    (a) Flying airplanes
    (b) Singing music
    (c) Gathering shoes

4. Computer System is also useful in the following places EXCEPT ___________.
    (a) Car Terminus for counting of cars
    (b) On the Major Road for Traffic Control

(c)   Refuse Dump

5. Computer System is used at home to ______.

(a) Play music

(b) Praying

(c) Walking

6. Computer system can also be used in the ________

(a) Court

(b) Gutter

(c) Toilet

7. Students can used computer to do their ________

(a) Eating

(b) Examinations

(c) Socks

8. In the ______ computer is used for Sales Records.

(a) Schools

(b) Court

(c) Super Market

9. ________use computer to do Business transactions.

(a) Mosques

(b) Church

(c) Banks

10.   Computer is useful in all areas of life. Yes Or No

CHAPTER FIVE

Practical Pages

Trace the following Parts of Computer with Pencil

Color where necessary

Practical Class 1

Computer System

<u>**Class Activity**</u>

A. Mention 5 parts of Computer

(1) ______________________________

(2) ______________________________

(3) ______________________________

(4) ______________________________

(5) ______________________________

B. Circle each of these computer parts in the diagram below

    (i)   Keyboard

    (ii)   CPU

    (iii)   Monitor Screen

    (iv)   Mouse

    (v)   Monitor Stand

Mark Scored: ________

Practical Class 2

**Trace the picture below with pen and color**

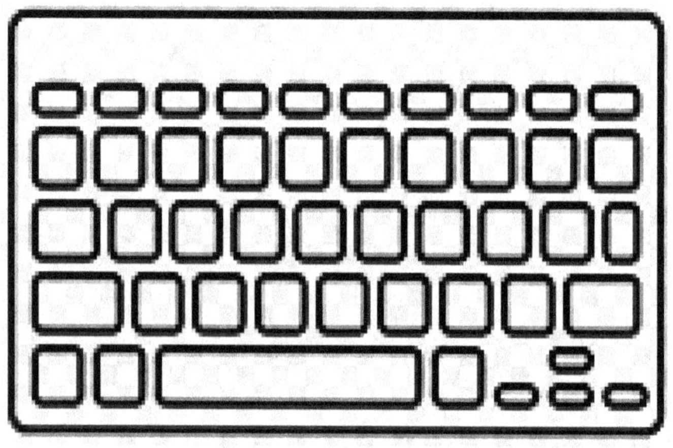

**This is a Keyboard**

It has many __________

The longest key is called ____________

I can trace it with my pencil.

I can color it with my crayon.

_**- Mark Scored: _____**_

<u>*Practical Class 3*</u>

Trace the picture below with pen and color

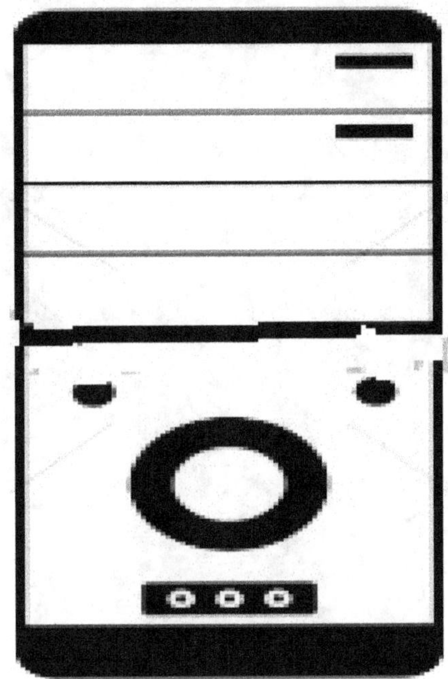

This is Central Processing Unit (CPU)

It has a disk _____________

It has a __________ button

I can trace it with my pencil.

I can color it with my crayon.

Mark Scored: _____

<u>Practical Class 4</u>

Trace the picture below with pen and color

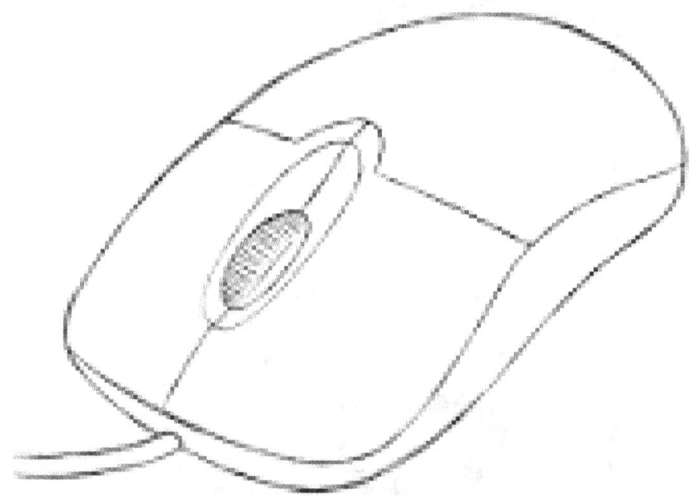

This is a Mouse.

It has two ___________

It can stand on a Mouse ___________

II can trace it with my pencil.

I can color it with my crayon.

- *Mark Scored:* ______

Trace the picture below with pen and color

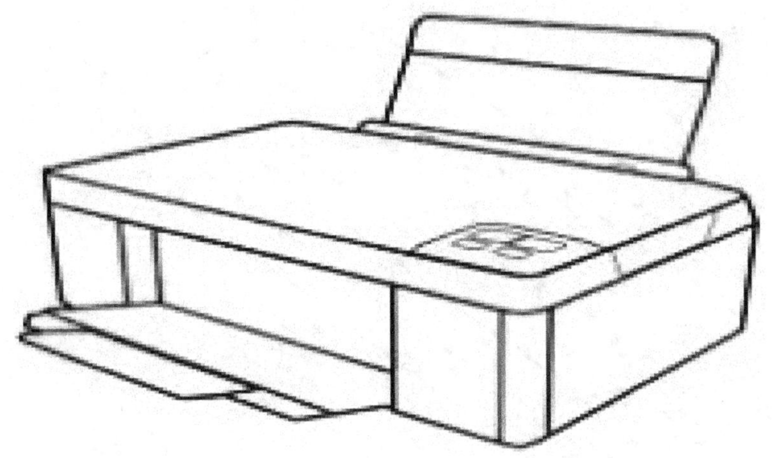

This is a _______________

   (a) Printer

   (b) Scanner

   (c) Mouse

It is used for _______________

   (a) Writing

   (b) Sitting

   (c) Printing documents

Mark Scored: _______

Practical Class 6

Trace the picture below with pen and color

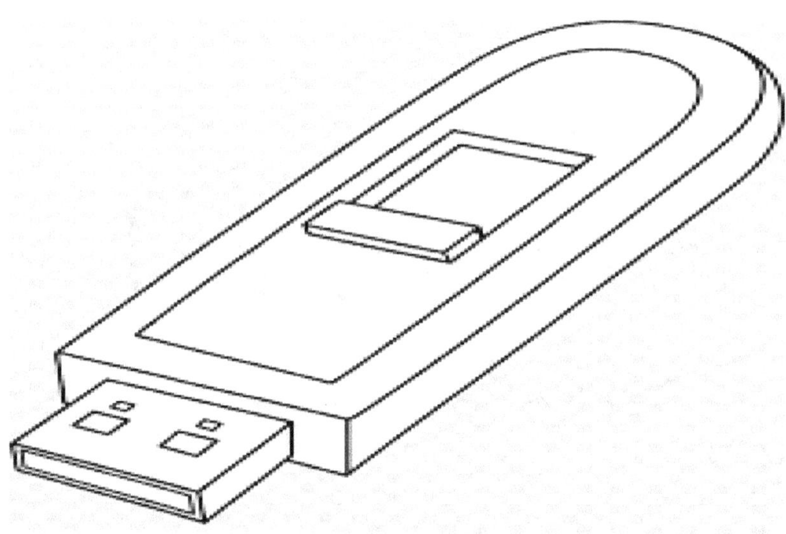

_This is a ___________

    (a)   **CPU**

    (b)   **Flash Drive**

    (c)   **Joystick**

_It is used for ______________

    (d)   **Storage of data**

    (e)   **Sweeping the floor**

    (f)   **Writing documents**

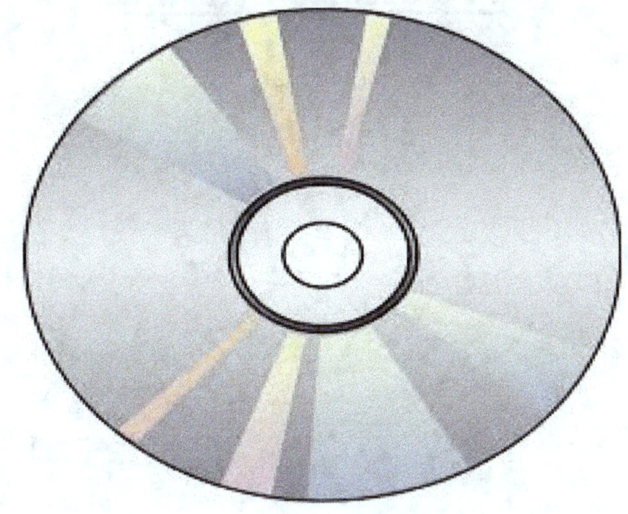

This is a __________

    (a)   **Keyboard**

    (b)   **Flash Drive**

    (c)   **Compact Disc (CD)**

It is used for _______________

    (d)   **Storage of data**

    (e)   **Scanning documents**

    (f)   **Writing documents**

Mark Scored: ______

Practical Class 8

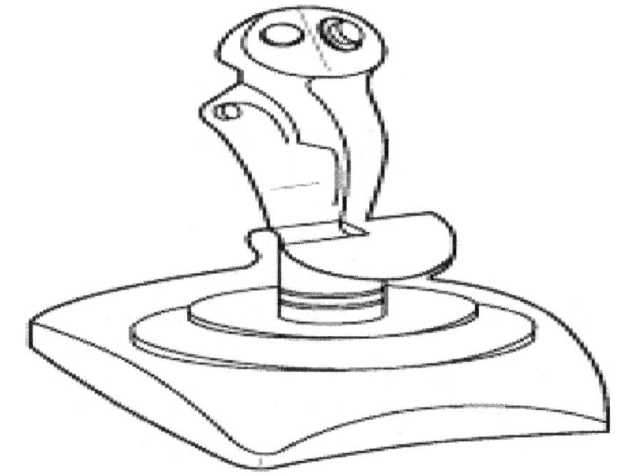

This is a __________

    (a)   Pencil

    (b)   Mouse

    (c)   Joystick

It is used for ______________

    (d)   Drawing

    (e)   Storage

    (f)   Cleaning

Mark Scored: ______

Practical Class 9

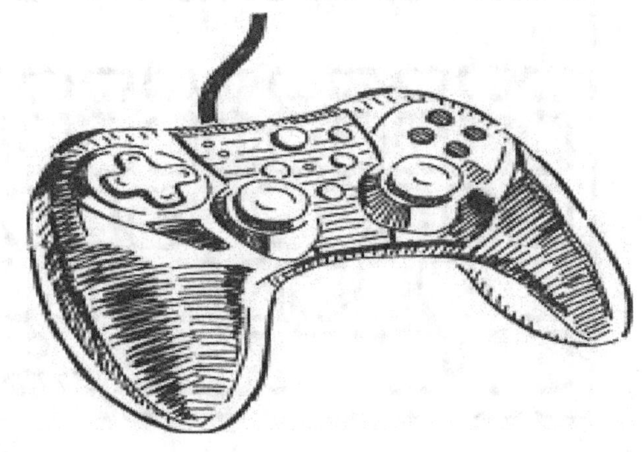

This is a _______________

    (a)   **Games Pad**

    (b)   **Cassette**

    (c)   **Joystick**

It is used for _______________

    (a)   **Playing games**

    (b)   **Picking objects**

    (c)   **Typing documents**

Mark Scored: _______

This is a __________

    (a)   Games Pad

    (b)   Cassette

    (c)   Keyboard

It is used for _____________

    (d)   Typing Data

    (e)   Picking objects

    (f)   Storing Data

Mark Scored: ________

GENERAL QUESTIONS

1. Computer is an ______ machine.

    (a) light

    (b) electronic

    (c) spinning

2. Computer makes use of ______ to work.

    (a) candle

    (b) fuel

    (c) electricity

3. Computer processes data through ______ device.

    (a) Input

    (b) Processing

    (c) Output

4. Computer accepts data through ______ device.

    (a) Output

    (b) Input

(c) processing

5. _______ is an example of Input Device.

(a) Speaker

(b) Mouse

(c) Monitor

6. ________ is an example of Output Device.

(a) Monitor

(b) Joystick

(b) Light Pen

7. Computerized Devices make use of

______ to function.

(a) fuel

(b) water

(c) electricity

8. Computerized Devices work _______.

(a) slow

(b) faster

(c) without human intervention

9. _______ is an example of Computerized Devices.

   (a) Washing Machine

   (b) Blackboard

   (c) Table

10. Liquid Dispenser and Fax Machine are examples of ___ Devices.

   (a) Magnetic

   (b) Computerized

   (c) Speedy

11. Computerized Devices are used in many ___________.

   (a) homes

   (b) tables

   (c) skies

12. This is a __________

(a) Monitor

(b) Scanner

(c) Mouse

13. This is a _______

(a) Scanner

(b) Joystick

(c) Hard Disk

14. This is a _______

(a) Printer

(b) Circle

(c) Compact Disc

15. This is a _____

(a) Monitor

(b) Memory Card

(c) Mouse

16. This is a _________

(a) Flash Drive

(b) CPU

(c) VDU

17. Monitor looks like _____

(a) Soap

(b) Television Set

(c) Ball

18. _________ looks like a rat moving on a table

   (a) Keyboard

   (b) Mouse

   (c) Typewriter

19. CPU looks like _______

   (a) Brief Case

   (b) Photocopy Machine

   (c) Table

20. Keyboard looks like _____

   (a) hand

   (b) Typewriter

   (c) Video Player

21. Compact Disc look like a ____

   (a) Motor

   (b) Rat

   (c) Stereo Disc

22. Joystick looks like a ______

    (a) Banana

    (b) Car Gear

    (c) Bell

23. The outer cover of the monitor is called __.

    (a) Cloth

    (b) Casin

    (c) Colour

24. One of the places where computers are found is

    ________.

    (a) Mansion

    (b) Mantle

    (c) Mosque

25. Computer is taught as a subject in _____.

    (a) Schools

    (b) Prisons

    (c) Palace

26. Computer is switched through _________.

    (a) Steering

    (b) Power Button

    (c) cables

27. Mouse looks like a _______ moving on a table.

    (a) Ball

    (b) Basket

    (c) Rat

28. Computer games can be played on computer using _________

    (a) Joystick

    (b) Remote Control

    (c) PS-2

29. One of the games which can be played on the Computer is _______.

    (a) Footmat

(b) Colour-Match

(c) Snake and Ladder

30. USP is an acronym for ___________.

(a) Unit Sport Port

(b) Universal Serial Port

(c) Uninterrupted Split Port

31. Printer is one of the examples of ______ devices.

(a) Output

(b) Processing

(c) Input

32. __________ is printed through Printer.

(a) Softcopy

(b) Hard disk

(c) Hardcopy

33. One of the examples of hardcopy is __________.

    (a) Ms Word

    (b) Textbook

    (c) CorelDraw

34. The materials printed for us to read

are called ____________.

    (a) hardcopy

    (b) Softcopy

    (c) photocopy

35. We use _____ cable to join printer to the CPU.

    (a) VDU

    (b) DVD

    (c) USB

36. Another name for CPU is _________.

    (a) System Unit

    (b) Basic Unit

    (c) Brain Unit

37. Computer processes data into useful

    information through _______.

    (a) Input Unit

    (b) Output Unit

    (c) Processing Unit

38. Computer data and information are stored

    in _______ Unit.

    (a) Processing

    (b) Storage

    (c) Input

39. Computer Keyboard has many __________

on its board.

(a) Keys

(b) Buttons

(b) Press

40. Computer can work ______than any other

machines.

(a) slower

(b) faster

(c) nicer

ANSWER TO QUESTIONS

1.   B

2.   C

3.   B

4.   B

5.   B

6.   A

7.   C

8.   B

9.   A

10.   B

11.   A

12.   B

13.   C

14.   C

15.   A

16.   B

17.   B

18.   B

19.   A

20.   B

21.   C

22.   B

23.   B

24.   C

25.   A

26.   B

27.   C

28.   A

29.   C

30.   B

31.   A

32.   C

33.   B

34.   A

35.   C

36.   A

37.   C

38.   B

39.   A

40.   B

About the BOOK

The book COSMOPOLITAN COMPUTER COMPUTERS FOR BASIC SCHOOLS (SERIES) is a computer book written in a familiar manner to make the teaching and learning of Computer fascinating, understandable and attractive to both teachers and the pupils.

The book is also written in a colorful, education and insightful manner in order to make the subject of computer fascinating and also make the pupil to be cosmopolitan as far as the knowledge of computer is concerned.

The Author: Samuel Olushola Adedokun has written the book in such a manner understandable for the pupils in Basic Schools.

About the AUTHOR

SAMUEL OLUSHOLA ADEDOKUN is computer tutor who is versatile in the teaching of Computer Education in Basic Schools. He has taught in different schools in his country of residence. He is so committed to making sure that every pupils in Basic Schools get a cosmopolitan knowledge about Computer Education in any country of the world.

<u>SOCIA MEDIA HANDLES</u>

E-mails: consultingdivineconnection@gmail.com
Connectionconsultingdivine@gmail.com

Facebook: facebook/divine connection consulting

Instagram: adedokunsamulgmail

Twitter: @divineconnection Consulting

YouTube: DivineConnect TV

LinkedIn: Adedokun Olushola Samuel